MW00412508

Be Safe, Be Responsible: Understanding Dog-Dog & Dog-Human Communication

Nikki Ivey

ISBN-10:1490354573
ISBN-13:9781490354576

DEDICATION

Dogs are known as man's best friend and yet, we don't spend the time we should to truly understand their ways. This book is dedicated to you, the reader, who understands the importance of knowing how your best friend communicates so you can develop a relationship that will flourish throughout the years.

CONTENTS

ACKNOWLEDGMENTS

I want to thank Compactio™ Marketing for putting DogSpeak on the map. I want to thank my manager, Britteny Watson, for all of her hard work and dedication. Thank you to all my wonderful clients and students from around the world that have embraced DogSpeak™ and embraced the idea that you can truly make a difference in dog's lives by learning more about your dog and not just going through the motions with your heart. I'm proud of each and every one of you! Most importantly, I want to thank God for giving me the gift of understanding dogs and working with them, as well as having the patience to teach their owners. I'm thoroughly blessed each time I get to make a difference in their lives.

CHAPTER 1
DOG COMMUNICATION AND LANGUAGE

Dog Language is the utilization of specific body postures, noises and actions that help a dog to communicate effectively with other dogs and people. A dog's sole purpose for using dog language is to avoid conflict. Dogs perceive conflict differently than humans. Dog conflict may be perceived when another dog or human plays too rough, when a human, animal or object approaches too quickly, or when a human is loud or overly confrontational. Conflict can also be caused by elements in the environment such as thunder, fireworks, cameras or cars. Avoiding conflict does not always mean a dog is trying to thwart a fight, it means he is trying to pacify what makes him uncomfortable. Dogs need to learn how to appropriately communicate with other dogs and conversely, humans need to know how to read this language.

Calming Signals

There are **three levels of calming signals**

dogs use in order to communicate. These levels range from passive (Level 1) to aggressive (Level 3). Dog language can be difficult to detect and decipher until you are introduced to it. After which, it becomes obvious and even entertaining.

Dogs offer a *behavior* when they want something, like a treat, a toy, or play. They offer a *signal* when they want to solicit a calming effect.

Level 1 – Passive Signals

Level 1 is the most innate level of signals used, *only if* the dog has had a chance to practice dog language. Many dogs lack proficient communication skills because they do not get adequate interaction with other dogs. Although born with the ability to communicate, dogs must practice these skills on a regular basis. If not, they lack the confidence to control a situation that may escalate into conflict. Dogs with insufficient language skills usually skip Level 1 signals.

Head Turn:

This is the most commonly used signal. A dog will slowly turn his head from side to side, avoiding eye contact. He may do this for many seconds before attempting another signal in order to give the conflict a chance to appropriately diminish. As rescuers, you probably see this signal often when trying to photograph a dog because many dogs see cameras as a conflict. Use this signal to calm a dog that is nervous, shy or overly excited.

Body Turn:

A dog will turn his entire body from a frontal position and show you his side or he may turn all the way around and show you his rear. This is another great signal that you can use to help calm down a dog. This is the most effective technique when dealing with a jumping dog.

Eye Aversion:

This is when a dog will avert his eyes away from you without necessarily turning his head or body. You will often see dogs do this when you have a dog's face in your hands, and he cannot turn his head.

Sit:

Dogs will sit when dealing with a new dog, an overly excited dog or a human who is being too forceful. Many times a sit will become a default behavior when a dog does not know what else to do to appease a situation. To understand if the action is a signal or a behavior, look at the rest of the body. If it is used as a signal, the dog will use it with another signal like turning the head or averting the eyes. If it is a behavior, the dog will sit and look towards the other dog or human. This is a great signal to use when dealing with nervous or shy dogs. Instead of sitting, I recommend squatting so it is easier to move away or closer to the dog depending on the response he is giving you. When you squat, you will always use another signal like head turning, body turning or averting the eyes.

Down:

This signal is not as common as the previous. Little dogs are more likely to use the down as a signal or behavior than a larger dog. Dogs with a high level of confidence will also be more likely to use this signal. Like a sit, you will see other behaviors combined with it. Always look at the rest of the body and in what context the down is being used.

Bow:

This can be used as a signal or as a behavior. When used as a signal, a dog will go into the bow position where his front legs are stretched out in front and his bottom is up in the air. However, unlike a play bow where a dog will jump from side-to-side quickly as a play invitation, a dog will remain stationary when using a bow as a calming signal. When it is a signal, you will often times see it mixed with another signal like averting eyes or turning the head. Dogs that have very good dog skills will sometimes use a bow as a signal and behavior at the same time. He may want another dog to play, but if the other dog is anxious, the bowing dog may offer a calming signal to relieve the tension of the encounter. You can use this as a signal yourself, but you may feel silly doing it. I recommend using the more natural signals like head and body turns, eye aversion and sitting/squatting.

Quick Licks:

This signal is difficult to see until you are used to spotting it. A quick lick is when the tongue comes out of the mouth and in a very quick motion licks the nose and then quickly moves back in. A dog that uses this will do it several times in a row to try and get his point across. Quick licks will also be combined with other signals.

Raised Paw:

This signal is not used as often as the others. When a dog is using this as a signal, he will slightly raise the paw and use another signal with it. Keep in mind you must read the entire body in order to identify this as a calming signal. If the dog is a pointer, for instance, a raised paw may mean the dog is simply pointing something.

Doing Something Else (Ignoring):

A dog will do this when he wants to extinguish a behavior. He may sniff the ground, urinate and/or completely ignore what it is he wants to extinguish. Many people see this as a dog being stubborn but in most cases, the dog is trying to calm a situation. For example, your dog, Jake, is playing in the yard and you call him to you. He does not listen to you the first three times. Why? He may not know the command. Or, if he does, you could be using a harsh tone that he views as a conflict. If the latter is correct, Jake will ignore you and wait for you to calm down.

Yawning:

Dogs yawn for two reasons. He may yawn because he is tired or as a signal to calm a situation or himself. Look at what context the yawn is being used to help you decide if it is a signal or a behavior. On occasion, a dog will use this with other signals.

Curving:

When meeting a new dog or sometimes, a new person, a dog will curve towards the object to show calmness and friendliness. This is where dogs will greet one another by smelling their rear ends or genitalia. This seems rude to us, but in reality, meeting face-to-face is inappropriate and confrontational in a dog's world. Many dogs, especially puppies, are not good at this signal due to a lack of experience and maturity. Poor greeting signals will often start a scuffle. Use this method when meeting a new dog. Walking up to the dog from the side, and curving to greet him. Do not approach a strange dog from the front. And I suggest that you never bend over a dog that you are unfamiliar with its temperament.

Splitting Up:

If you have ever had a dog sit or stand between you and another person, (i.e. while cuddling on the couch with your significant other), you have probably seen this signal. Many people think this is a cute gesture of jealousy, however the dog actually sees this as a conflict and is trying to *literally* split you apart. During play, dogs will do this when they sense other dogs' rough play will cause a fight. Confident, experienced dogs will walk between two dogs, and will stay with the offending dog until it redirects, much like an umpire during a sporting match. This signal takes a lot of practice as most dogs lack the consistency, confidence and follow-through to do it properly. The more a dog has a chance to interact with other dogs, the better he will become.

Level 2 - Less Passive Signals

Level 2 signals are less passive and very easily recognized. Many humans become uncomfortable when they see Level 2 signals, often labeling a dog as vicious. Dogs will use Level 2 signals if they do not, 1. Have confidence, 2. The time to use Level 1 signals, or 3. To articulate to the other dog that his patience is growing thin.

Growling:

A dog will give a low growl to let another dog or person know he is uncomfortable. This means that the dog is *trying* to control a potentially conflicting situation. When growling is used as a signal it is mixed with other signals such as a head turn. If growling is a behavior, other signals are not used, and the dog's posture will be stiff and he will stare at the person or dog ahead of him. If you have a patient dog with good dog language, he will often try Level 1 signals first. If using Level 1 signals is not effective, he will be forced to escalate to Level 2. For example, if a family pet is constantly harassed by a child at home, (say the child is crawling all over him, chasing him down, getting in his face, etc.), and the dog's Level 1 signals are being ignored, the dog will be forced to escalate to Level 2. When the dog growls at the child, the family scolds the dog instead of educating the child, or they improperly assume the dog is vicious, and re-home the dog or worse. This scenario is one that occurs all too often. It is important to know whether the dog had previously displayed Level 1 signals prior to the growl, and before jumping to Level 2.

Snarling:

A snarl occurs when a dog pulls his lips up and shows his teeth. This signal is often used with a low growl and always with a Level 1 signal such as a quick lick, head turn or eye aversion. Many fearful dogs with no confidence will resort to this behavior immediately when faced with an uncomfortable situation. Dogs with confidence will use a snarl if they do not have time to use a Level 1 signal, (i.e. when another dog is suddenly in his face). Like the growl, if it is not mixed with other signals, it is being given as a behavior with the possibility of turning into aggression.

<u>Level 3 – Aggressive Signals</u>

Level 3 is considered the Aggressive Level. When a dog uses Level 3 signals, it does not mean he is vicious, it just means that the signals are much more noticeable to the untrained eye. Dogs use this Level when Levels 1 and 2 did not work or he does not have the patience or skills to do Levels 1 and 2 first. Level 3 signals are very obvious and often make people nervous. Because of their lack of understanding, they will often punish or correct a dog for offering Level 3 signals. This will normally make the dog resort to level 3 faster than usual, because of the association of correction or punishment when another dog gets too close. Level 3 signals can also be behaviors from a dog that is being a bully so you must read the dog's entire body to understand.

Muzzle Grab:

A muzzle grab occurs when a dog attempts to place his mouth over another dog's muzzle. This may be a sign of dominance because it places another dog into a submissive position. Humans sometimes use a version of this by purchasing head halters that go over the muzzle of their dog. This is placed into the aggressive level, because there is physical contact between the dogs. Though the dog giving signals does not intend to cause harm, the dog receiving the muzzle grab will oftentimes get a cut on the bridge of the muzzle because the skin is thin in this area. This behavior is acceptable when the previous two levels have not worked. Most young puppies experience this at least once in their life. If you observe a dog is not respecting Level 1 and 2 signals, you should correct the disrespectful dog—not the dog giving the signals.

Snapping:

When giving this signal a dog will snap towards whatever needs calming, and then back away quickly. This occurs when humans who do not understand that the dog has been displaying Level 1 and 2 signals and continue to place the dog in an uncomfortable and stressful environment. When the conflict is not resolved, then the dog will escalate to snapping. A dog at this level is usually snapping out of fear, or lacks the confidence and maturity to disengage emotionally from what is causing the fear. Essentially, all he wants is to avoid conflict and to make something go away. The dog that uses snapping as a behavior, will often not back down after snapping. This is the difference between a dog using proper dog language or getting caught up in his fear turning dangerously aggressive. This is also the number one signal that is used when a dog has no confidence or does not understand the first two levels.

Biting:

Often times biting is a dog's last resort when other signals have not worked. Like a dog that uses a snap, dogs with low confidence or language skills often bite instead of offering Level 1 or 2 signals. If a dog is using this as a signal, the dog will often bite and then back off. I define a bite as a snap with contact. A signal bite is different than a warning bite. A dog that is using the bite as a warning behavior will hold and shake its victim and not back down. A hold and shake will cause more damage than a signal bite and release.

When observing any Level 3 signals, you must not jump to conclusions. Level 3 signals do not necessarily mean that the dog is vicious and cannot be rehabilitated. You must evaluate the dog carefully to adequately evaluate why the dog used this level of signals or behavior. Is he offering Level 1 and 2 first or is he going immediately to Level three? The more you observe, the more competent you will be at evaluating the dog.

Final Words on Dog Signals

To dogs, dog signals are the bases to living a conflict-free life. As pack animals, avoiding conflict means harmony among the pack. For your dog, avoiding conflict is more important than being obedient as obedience is only important to the human. Keep this in mind when out in public with your dog and especially at a dog park.

CHAPTER 2
VARIOUS SIGNALS

Dogs give other dogs and humans various signals that help them communicate. These signals are not necessarily calming signals, and are typically easy to recognize.

Tail Wag:

This is the most misunderstood signal. A tail wag does not always mean "happy dog". A tail wag means a dog is aroused in one form or another. When evaluating what a particular tail wag means look at the entire body for confirmation. Also, take a dog's breed into consideration. Many dogs do not have tails, and others normally have a stiff or curled tail.

If a dog's tail is **slow and relaxed**, the dog is comfortable in the current situation. I also refer to this as the "flag" wag, because it often looks like a flag blowing in the wind.

A **high, stiff and slow wag** means the dog is being challenging or taking a defensive posture. If it is not moving, the dog could be trying to calm another dog. I refer to this wag as a "stick in low wind."

A **high, stiff and fast wag** means a dog is highly aroused. Arousal can come from a variety of sources. This is also known as the "stick in a hurricane" wag.

A fast to moderate and relaxed wags means a dog is happy and comfortable. Often times the wag will make a circle, which is why I refer to this as a "circle wag."

If a dog has a **low/no wag,** the dog is uncomfortable from fear or nervousness. A low/no wag can also come from pain. Sometimes the tail will be tucked between the legs.

Raised Hackles:

At some point you will see the fur on the back or neck of a dog stand up. This is a natural response to arousal. Arousal can be from excitement, being unsure, low confidence, and/or aggression. A dog that has his hackles raised is not necessarily getting ready to attack. You must always read the entire body of a dog to really understand what he is trying to communicate. Again, you must be aware of the breed. Breeds such as Rhodesian ridgebacks have raised fur all the time.

Shake Off:

Shake offs are used as a "release" which can denote the beginning of play or the end of a sequence of events, (i.e. after a long introduction, a dog shakes off to show he is ready for play).

Barking:

Dog use barking as a vocal way to communicate. Keep in mind a mastiff and a Chihuahua will have different low-pitched barks:

A **high-pitched bark** indicates excitement, heavy arousal, fearfulness or nervousness.

A **low-pitched bark** is used for warning or frustration.

Distance Increasing Signals

These signals are used to increase the distance between a dog and a conflict. When a dog is uncomfortable with something (i.e. another dog that is too close), he will use these signals as a way to express his desire to be away from the conflict.

Whining, Yelping and Crying:

These will often come from insecure puppies or dogs that are unable to use calming signals properly. Crying and whining is a vocal way of demonstrating frustration and not used for distance increasing. Yelping can be associated with pain, (think about the last time you accidentally stepped on your dog's tail).

CHAPTER 3
HUMANS CAN SPEAK DOG

Humans Can Speak Dog!

Humans are capable of communicating with dogs by using these same signals. Whether you have a dog that is afraid, nervous or outgoing, you can calm him by using these same signals. Practice using these signals with your own dog until they become second nature to you. Start by seeing how well your dog responds to them. How well they respond will tell you how well they know dog language, as well as help you improve your own skills. Use only Level 1 signals with your dog and be sure to be confident and consistent!

A **head turn** is easy to use with a jumping or nervous dog. Be sure to completely ignore the dog (no touching or talking) while using this signal.

A **body turn** is a great way to deal with a jumping dog. When the dog sits for 3-5 seconds, verbally acknowledge the dog for being good. If the dog jumps again, turn your body and ignore him. If the dog is causing you pain from jumping, ignore the dog and walk to another room.

Use a **sit or squat** with a nervous or fearful dog (if they are not oversized.) Always keep your body turned to the side.

In order for **yawning** to work, you must be consistent. Mix this with another signal such as a head turn. You can use this signal to your advantage when dealing with a nervous or shy dog. For instance, if a dog is afraid of thunderstorms, make sure the dog is near you. Simply ignore the dog (do not coddle), and yawn from time to time. You may see the dog begin to yawn back. He is trying to calm himself.

Again, **curving** should always be used when meeting a new dog. Approach the dog from the side, and curve to greet. Do not approach a dog head on.

Split ups should not be overused. It is essential that you are confident and consistent when walking in between two dogs. Follow-though is crucial in order for this signal to work. For example, if your dog is barking at a door, confidently position yourself between the dog and the door. Move your body toward the dog until it redirects. Do not talk or touch the dog. If the dog gets around you and returns to the door, do not panic. Simply start over

CHAPTER 4
RESOURCES

I hope that this book has brought you much-needed education in order to help you understand how your dog communicates with other dogs and with humans. As an owner, I want you to start practicing reading signals by going to the dog park, without your dog, or by watching your own dogs interact. By practicing you will be able to see the signals faster in order to respond appropriately in a timely manner. By understanding dog communication you can help your dog become a better dog in dealing with conflict and stress. Below are some resources that will further your success with your dog on becoming confident and clear when communicating.

I encourage you, if you have not, take our seminar, "Be Safe, Be Responsible: Understanding Dog-Dog & Dog-Communication" through E-Training For Dogs. By taking the seminar, which includes over 50 videos, you will understand dog language faster.

For questions please contact Nikki at info@dogspeak101.com

Get Nikki's latest books through Amazon.com

Website: For the latest DogSpeak news, and to see how Nikki can help you privately, visit www.dogspeak101.com

E-Training for Dogs: Bring Nikki's seminars, including "When Love Isn't Enough," to your home! www.e-trainingfordogs.com

Facebook: Get the latest news from DogSpeak! www.facebook.com/DogSpeak101

YouTube: Check out exclusive training videos! www.youtube.com/DogSpeak102

55538376R00019

Made in the USA
Lexington, KY
26 September 2016